Make More Money

Make More Money

Brian Tracy

Published 2018 by Gildan Media LLC
aka G&D Media
www.GandDmedia.com

FIRST EDITION 2018

Front Cover design by David Rheinhardt of Pyrographx

Interior design by Meghan Day Healey of Story Horse, LLC

Library of Congress Cataloging-in-Publication Data is available upon request

ISBN: 978-1-7225-0019-1

10   9   8   7   6   5   4   3   2   1

Contents

Introduction

Welcome to *Make More Money*, the easy-to-follow habits of successful millionaires and billionaires.

Over the years, I've given more than 5,000 talks and seminars in 72 countries, to more than five million people, on the subjects of personal and business success. I have spent decades studying the life stories of the most successful people in our world, both currently and historically, and I found that they all have certain characteristics and habits in common. This is what you will learn in this book.

An Eye Opener—
Who Becomes Wealthy?

et me tell you a quick story. When I began speaking and conducting seminars some years ago, I received a call from the president of a large international company. He was going to have about 800 of his business partners at their annual convention.

He asked me if I would come and speak on the secrets of success of self-made millionaires, and how people could become wealthy in one generation. I said, "Of course."

When you are a new speaker, you are willing to speak to anybody on any subject, and you always hold yourself out as an expert.

However, when I hung up the phone, I realized that I didn't really know very much about millionaires. I was in my late 30s. I had always wanted to be a millionaire. My goal was to be a millionaire by the time I was 30, and then, by the time I was 35. But as the years passed, I was no closer. I was beginning to lose hope.

So, to prepare for this talk, I began to read the research on self-made millionaires. I found that there was an enormous amount of study that had been done on the subject. Tens of thousands of self-made millionaires had been analyzed and interviewed. These were people who had started with nothing, and in one generation became millionaires, and often billionaires.

What I found was that they all had certain traits and behaviors in common. Two months later, I was ready. I got up and I gave a speech on the qualities, characteristics, habits and behaviors of self-made millionaires.

The speech was so successful that I was asked to give it over and over again, by groups and organizations all over the world. It started off as a one hour speech and then became 90 minutes, and then a half day, and finally it became a full day program, complete with workbooks and exercises.

Something Amazing Happened

Then, the most amazing thing happened. Within five years, I was myself a millionaire. I literally went from rags to non-rags, as I say. By practicing what I was preaching, by simply repeating these ideas and strategies over and over again, I programmed myself to think differently about my financial potential. I found myself doing more and more of the things that self-made millionaires do, and less and less of the things that poor people, or people with average incomes do. And my whole life changed.

You Can Do It Too

In this book, I'm going to give you some facts, figures and data, and explain some of the habits, behaviors, and thinking tools of self-made millionaires. I will tell you some of the practical things that they do every day to become wealthy and stay wealthy.

Let's begin. The statistics this year (2015) are really quite remarkable. In the year 1900, just over a century ago, there were only 5,000 millionaires. Today, there are about ten million, six hundred thousand millionaires in the U.S. alone, and another 20,000,000 worldwide, many of them coming from poor countries.

More people are becoming millionaires faster today than ever before.

Starting With Nothing

Eighty percent of these millionaires are self-made, first generation. When I began my research, there were no billionaires at all. In 2015, according to *Forbes Magazine* and other studies, there were 1,845 billionaires in the world. Each year, more and more people are becoming billionaires. Just to get to the *Forbes 400*, the 400 richest people in America, you have to have a net worth of more than $1.6 billion dollars.

When I began following it in 1980, you could get on to the Forbes 400 of the richest people with 200 million dollars. 66% of self-made billionaires started with nothing. The others inherited money from their families and from a variety of other sources, but 66% of the richest people in the world started off with nothing. They started off with common backgrounds, sometimes limited educations. Sometimes they are immigrants with no language skills. Sometimes they struggled for years before they finally discovered the unique set of circumstances that enabled them to become wealthy, and maybe that's what you'll do after this program. The Sources of Wealth

The primary sources of wealth are businesses, of all kinds—manufacturing, shipping, distribution, oil, gas, real estate, food and restaurants. Businesses are by far the greatest generators of wealth.

Sometimes I ask my audiences, "How many people here work on straight commission?" There is usually a pause while some people look uncomfortable, and then maybe ten or 15 percent raise their hands.

Create Value

Then I say, "Here's the real truth: everybody works on straight commission. Everybody gets a part of the value that they create. If you create more value, you earn more money. Either your current boss or some other boss will eagerly pay you a percentage of the additional value you are creating."

I always say that good employees, good people in any field, are free, plus a profit. They contribute vastly more value than they are paid, and they contribute even more value to their company than they cost. They are essential in helping their companies to make a profit.

This is why every company is successful to the degree to which it continues to hire talented people who contribute more than they cost.

Microsoft™ has 120,000 employees, and almost every one of them contributes more than they are costing, so Microsoft™ continues to earn billions and billions of dollars, and Bill Gates is the richest man in the world. This is the same with Google, Apple, Facebook and all successful companies.

Real Estate Riches

The second primary source of wealth is real estate. They say, "Real estate—they're not making any more of it. You can get rich in real estate." But this is not always true. People go broke in real estate every year.

I met a gentleman recently who sold his manufacturing business for $50 million dollars. He came in to see me with a business proposition. His idea was not very attractive, and he did not seem to be either happy or successful.

He told me an interesting story. He said, "When I sold my business for $50 million dollars, which I had spent more than 20 years building up, everyone told me to invest in real estate."

So he did. But he didn't know very much about real estate or commercial property. He ended up investing in real estate until his money was all gone.

So just as people make money in real estate, people also lose money in real estate. There are many people worth hundreds of millions of dollars in real estate one year, and a few years later they're broke and they're back working for wages.

The critical thing about real estate is that most people are successful at it when they focus single-mindedly only on real estate and nothing else.

Other people who are successful in real estate are those who take their money from their successful businesses and invest it with real estate experts who know what they are doing. Real estate can be a primary source of wealth but only if you do it right.

Money and Investments

The third major source of wealth is banking and finance. It's absolutely amazing how many people in the Forbes 400 run or build banks or are in venture capital or equity financing of some kind, including life insurance, and other ways of investing and using capital.

Someone once said to me, "If you want to make peanuts, grow peanuts. If you want to make money, sell money." People in the financial services industry, the money business, are often some of the wealthiest people in the world. They earn a small or large piece of the value they create.

Technological Riches

Technology is the fourth major source of riches and one of the greatest creators of millionaires and billionaires in the world today. All kinds of people from around the world are pouring into Silicon Valley to find venture capital financing for hundreds and thousands of ideas based on new technology.

Last year they calculated that there are more than one million experts—techies, geeks—who are working today, together with others or alone, to find the next "killer app." There are more people looking to develop the next killer application for iPhones than there are farmers in the United States. And this trend will continue. Money in Energy Production The fifth major source of wealth is oil and gas. World energy needs continue to grow and expand, especially in fields such as fracking. At one time, more millionaires and billionaires came from the gas and oil field than came from any other industry. Business Success

The key to business success has always been the same. First of all, find a need and fill it. One of the great secrets of business success is that if you want to make a lot of money, find a pressing need that a lot of people have and solve it in an excellent way.

This is the most dependable way to succeed in a market economy. Find something that people want and need then give it to them better than anyone else, both as a company and as an individual.

The second key to business success is to sell something to someone. This is the most powerful business strategy. I call this SMS—Sell More Stuff. It's amazing how many people are trying to start businesses, raising capital, developing technologies and opening offices, but they're not making any sales.

The most successful companies in the world are the ones that sell more stuff all day long. You know the saying, "Nothing happens until a sale takes place."

Don't Lose Money

The third key to business success is "don't lose money." If you have the idea that you can lose a little money, you're probably going to lose a lot. The most successful people are those who are almost fanatical about not losing money.

My friend Phil Towne, a successful author and investor, wrote a bestselling book called *Rule Number One*. According to millionaires and billionaires, Rule Number One, is "don't lose money." Take your time. Get the facts. Do your due diligence. Prepare thoroughly. Consider your financial moves carefully in advance. Get your blueprint ready, and don't lose money.

J. Paul Getty was once the richest man in the world. He was the first real billionaire. He was once asked what the key was to becoming a billionaire. He said, "First of all, if I find a good business deal and I examine it carefully, and I decide to go into it, that's the starting point. Then I ask, "What is the worst thing that can possibly happen? How can I lose money in this deal? Then I focus all of my efforts on making sure that the worst does not happen, on not losing money."

One of my mentors told me that the great secret to success was to learn from the experts. He told me that I would never live long enough to learn all that I needed to learn by myself. These ideas come from the leading experts in wealth creation in the world today.

In this e-book, you will learn how to go deeper into the personalities and behaviors that enable some people to become so wealthy while so many others struggle with money all their lives.

Habits of Millionaires and Billionaires

Most self-made millionaires and billionaires have special habits that separate them from average people. Since fully 95% of your behaviors are determined by your habits, the key to success is to develop good habits and make them your masters. Your success will be determined more by your habits that by anything else. Your financial situation will be more a result of your habits than your education, your background or even the wealth you inherit.

Ten Habits You Can Develop

Let's look at the ten most important personal habits of wealthy people.

1. Hard Work and Self-Discipline

The number one habit, according to interviews with the *Forbes 400, the* richest people in America in 2015, is *hard work and self-discipline.*

When the self-made billionaires on the list were surveyed, and asked what they thought were the main reasons for their extraordinary success, 76% of these wealthy people attributed their success to hard work and self-discipline more than any other quality.

Thomas Stanley, author of *The Millionaire Next Door,* found in interviewing more than 1000 self-made millionaires, that according to 84% of them, hard work and self-discipline were the reasons they had been able to succeed and thrive in their industries. Napoleon Hill, author of *Think and Grow Rich,* after a lifetime of studying wealthy people, concluded that "Self-discipline IS the master key to riches."

No Short Cuts

There are no shortcuts to success. My friend Charlie Jones used to say, "Side roads are slide roads." Refuse to listen to anybody who tells you that it's possible to make a lot of money without hard, hard work, for a long, long time. Most billionaires have been working in their area of expertise for twenty years or more before they reached critical mass and broke into the billionaire ranks.

It seems that millionaires work approximately 60 hours per week, or more, and they work all the time they work, on high value activities.

Average people work 40 hours or less. 50% or more of their working time is wasted on idle chit-chat with coworkers, email and social media, coffee breaks and lunches, and general inefficiency. As a result, the average person actually works about 20 hours a week in terms of actually producing value.

Early to Rise

Millionaires, according to recent studies, usually rise before 6:00 AM. They get up approximately three hours before their first appointment or commitment for the day. When they get up, they get going immediately, following about five basic rituals, like exercise, reading, meditating, planning and preparing.

They carefully plan and organize their day so that by the time an average person has gotten up, the self-made millionaire or billionaire has been working for two or three hours. They don't waste time.

2. Use Your Time Well

Habit number two is that rich people allocate their time carefully on the most important things they can be doing at any time. Warren Buffet was recently asked about his biggest secret for success. He said, "My secret is simple; I say NO to virtually every request of my time. Whatever anybody wants, I just automatically say no. I say it early and often so that I can do just those few things that really make a difference." Steve Jobs said the same thing.

The first question we ask, if hard work and self-discipline are the most important habits for financial success, is this: "What one action will you take immediately to begin developing these habits?"

Later, I will give you some ideas you can use to develop those habits you desire, faster than you might think possible.

3. Clear Goals and Plans

The third habit of wealthy people is that they create and work from clear, written goals and plans. A person who builds a beautiful home has an excellent blueprint. A person who builds a beautiful piece of machinery has detailed engineering designs.

People who want to make a lot of money have clear, written goals and plans that they follow.

Wealthy people not only have goals in every part of their lives, 85% of millionaires, according to the recent research, have one big goal. Sometimes they call this a BHAG, which stands for Big Hairy Audacious Goal.

Napoleon Hill said in *Think and Grow Rich* that your life only begins to become great when you develop a *burning desire* to accomplish a *Major Definite Purpose*, the focal point where you concentrate all of your energies on the one goal that can have the greatest positive impact on your life. Whatever you're doing, whenever you're working, you're always thinking about how to achieve this one big goal.

The Great Discovery

What we have found in our thousands of courses and seminars with people worldwide is that as you work on one main goal, especially a financial goal; you start to make progress on all your other goals at the same time, almost without noticing.

Millionaires work from clear plans of action. They do their planning well in advance. Napoleon Hill once said, "All success comes from developing new plans when the old plans fail." Failing to plan is planning to fail. Unclear goals and plans are the major reason why people fail, waste time, and lose money.

Finally, we find that millionaires set measures and deadlines for each of their goals. They hold their own feet to the fire. They don't let themselves off the hook. They constantly monitor their progress.

In summary, rich people are clear about their goals and objectives. They work from clear, written plans of action. They continually set measures, benchmarks, standards and deadlines for their goals and then they work non-stop to achieve them.

Zig Ziglar used to say that, "If you will be hard on yourself, life will be easy on you. But if you insist upon being easy on yourself, life is going to be very hard on you."

4. Save Your Money

The fourth habit of self-made millionaires is that they are *frugal*. We talked about this before. They are careful with their money. Millionaires, especially on their way up, don't buy new houses. They don't buy second homes. They don't buy airplanes and boats. They don't even buy new cars. They buy good used cars and invest the money they save. They keep all of their money working.

David Bach, the author who wrote "The Automatic Millionaire," popularized what became known as "the latte factor." He said, "Instead of spending five dollars a day on a latte from Starbucks, just drink normal coffee and put that five dollars away. That's $25 per week; $100 per month, and if you do that throughout your career, you'll be worth more than a million dollars just investing that money in good mutual funds as you go along." Be careful with small amounts of money and soon you will have large amounts.

Foolish In Small Things

There is a Warren Buffet story about when he was once playing golf, and one of his friends said "Warren, I'll bet you a thousand dollars you can't get the ball onto the green from here."

They were just teeing off, and the green was far away, it may have been possible to hit it with one swing. But Warren looked down the fairway and then said "No. It's just not a good bet."

His friend said, "Come on Warren, a thousand dollars is pocket change to you—it's nothing."

Warren replied, "Foolish in small things, foolish in large things. It's not a good bet, and I'm not going to make it."

That's a great insight: foolish in small things, foolish in large things. Here is one of the major reasons why people retire poor. Resolve today not to be foolish in small things.

5. Study Every Detail

Habit number five is that millionaires examine every detail of the investment or expense before making a decision. Like many others, the biggest mistakes that I have ever made involved not doing enough due diligence; not enough research, not checking and double checking and triple checking before making a financial decision.

On the other hand, the best business decisions I ever made were those that were preceded by very careful research. Perhaps the most popular word in new business today is "validate." Validate everything before you invest your money or your time.

Millionaires do not like to lose money. It's an emotional issue for them. They feel that they work so hard for their money that the idea of losing it because of not checking makes them tense and irritable.

6. Learn to Love Saving Money

Habit number six is that millionaires focus on financial accumulation. They want to both make a lot of money and then keep a lot money. As a wealthy mentor once told me, "It is not how much you make that counts; it is how much you keep."

Most people want to "have fun, fun, fun, till their daddy takes their T-bird away." My friend Denis Waitley said that, "Top people are goal achieving, whereas average people commit all their time to tension relieving. They think all day about relaxing and having fun, watching TV, and socializing with their friends.

Millionaires think long-term, and they think about financial accumulation continually. The great discovery, perhaps the greatest of all time is that "You become what you think about most of the time."

If you think continually about getting and keeping money, about financial accumulation, you are going to accumulate vastly more than if you are always thinking about spending your money, buying new toys, and having a good time.

7. Become Highly Productive

The seventh habit of self-made millionaires is that they are highly productive and use their time well. This is one of the most important qualities of all.

I sometimes ask my audiences, "How many hours per day does Bill Gates have?" They will always answer "24." Then I ask them how many hours a day they have? They immediately see what I am saying.

Whether you're the richest or poorest person in the world, when you wake up each morning, you've got 24 fresh, beautiful, shiny new hours. You are the one who decides what to do with them. It is all a matter of your priorities.

The major reason that people are unproductive is that they don't set priorities, and as a result, they don't work on the most valuable uses of their time.

There are three keys to developing the habit of high productivity:

Number one, self-made millionaires and billionaires plan every day in advance. They don't do things unless they are planned.

Number two, they set clear priorities on their time. They think carefully. "If I could only do one thing today, which one activity would render me the greatest value? Which one activity would enable me to contribute the most?" And that's what they start on first thing.

Number three, self-made millionaires and billionaires focus and concentrate on the most valuable use of their time, all the time. Simply use the Warren Buffet rule: If it's not the most valuable use of your time, just say no.

8. Never Stop Learning

The eighth habit of millionaires is that they are always learning new ideas. They read, listen and learn continually. The average wealthy person spends about two or three hours a day reading and keeping current with what is going on in their field, and adding new information. They read one or two books a week. They read magazines and newsletters. They download the most important developments that are happening in their field that can affect their ability to earn more money.

Wealthy people watch very little television, usually less than one hour per day, and if they do watch it, they usually watch it On Demand or Netflix so they can watch at their convenience.

Unfortunately, poor people, unsuccessful people, watch about five hours of television a day, and some watch seven or eight. The first thing they do when they get up in the morning is to turn on the television. When they come home at night, the first thing they do is turn on the television.

The Wall Street Journal did a study of television watching and compared it with incomes. They found that the wealthiest people actually had their televisions in a separate room from their family room and dining room. They have to actually get up and go to that room to watch TV.

Poor people have the biggest television they can afford right in the center of their homes and they watch it all the time. Your television can make you rich or make you poor. If you turn it off, it can make you rich. Nature abhors a vacuum, especially a vacuum of time, and if you're not spending your time watching television, you'll probably do something more productive. You'll learn more things. You'll concentrate on developing your business. You'll engage in physical fitness activities, and even better, you'll spend more time with your family. Cutting down your television time and increasing your productive and family time is a simple formula for success.

9. Ask More Questions

Habit number nine, millionaires and billionaires ask a lot of questions and listen carefully to the answers. They say that Mark Zuckerberg of Facebook has a very high question to answer ratio five to one. He asks questions five times more often than he gives answers or orders.

When you see a picture of Mark Zuckerberg, he looks like a big curious kid. People around him say he's absolutely amazing. He keeps asking more and more penetrating questions to help people think better and better about their decisions.

What is it that unsuccessful people do? They talk continually. They say whatever they think, whenever they think it. They override and interrupt other people.

10. Take Intelligent Risks

Habit number ten is that rich people are willing to take risks to increase their wealth. In the recent Forbes Issue on self-made billionaires, they said that a major reason they became wealthy was because they, unlike their friends, were willing to take risks.

This doesn't mean that you jump out of an airplane without a parachute, or take foolish chances. There's an old joke that says that, "If at first you don't succeed, then skydiving is probably not for you."

But wealthy people are willing to take intelligent risks. They take knowledgeable, informed or calculated risks. They study the situation carefully before they make a decision or take action. There is always the possibility of failure but you can reduce the risk by doing more homework. Self-made millionaires and billionaires are willing to take risks with no guarantee of success.

The fact is that you only learn to succeed by failing and by learning from your failures. In fact, we say that there is no such thing as failure, only feedback.

Three Rules for Taking Risks

First, be willing to move out of your comfort zone. The comfort zone is probably the greatest single enemy of success. Most people become comfortable in their existing situation, and they resist every temptation to change or to try something new and different. To be successful, you must be willing to expand and try something more, bigger or better than you've ever done before.

Second, focus on the opportunity rather than on safety and security. Wealthy people are continually seeking opportunities to be, to have and to do more. Average people seek security. Top people seek opportunities.

Third, rich people supervise their investments carefully. They don't like to lose money, so they spend a lot of time thinking about their investments, and about how to deploy their money even more intelligently.

How to Develop New Habits

have written books and articles on the subject of new habit development. Let me give you a couple of ideas that you can use to develop any one of these habits.

Rule number one is to select only one habit at a time that can help you to be more successful. If you were to select a single habit that you would like to have, and then work on that habit for a month, until it became automatic, and then select a second habit, and develop that, in the course of a year you could develop ten to 12 new habits. With 12 new life-enhancing habits, you could transform your life.

But if you try to develop more than one habit at a time, you end up developing no habits at all. Working on multiple habits seems to short circuit the development of a single habit. Your job is to select just one habit that can help you to become more successful.

Start with Punctuality

Decide from today to be punctual. Only two percent of people are always punctual. This is not easy. It takes planning and organizing and leaving early for every appointment. Punctuality requires long-term thinking. It takes discipline. But when people are punctual, everybody notices. It seems that opportunities tend to flow toward people who have a reputation for punctuality.

Here is an interesting rule that can open or close doors for you. It is, "Never hire a person who arrives late for a job interview." Being habitually late seems to indicate a character flaw. No matter what the excuse they give, stuck in traffic, couldn't find the address, had an emergency at home, or whatever. It doesn't matter what the excuse, if a person comes late to a job interview, never hire them.

Just imagine how many job opportunities, and other opportunities, are silently closed just because a person did not leave a few minutes earlier for an important meeting. Don't let this happen to you.

Just resolve to be punctual for every appointment for the next 30 days. Vince Lombardi, the top football coach, was famous for what was called, "Lombardi time." Lombardi time meant 15 minutes early. So if the bus was scheduled to leave at 10:00 AM, the bus would actually depart at 9:45. If you weren't there early, you missed the bus and the next game. From now on, practice Lombardi time and be 15 minutes early for every appointment.

The Great Rule

Wolfgang von Goethe, the German writer and philosopher, once said, "Everything is hard before it's easy."

The development of new habits is hard, hard work, but once you've developed the habit, it becomes automatic and easy. Eventually, it becomes easier to behave consistent with the new habit than it was before. It becomes automatic.

My friend Ed Forman used to say that, "good habits are hard to form but easy to live with, while bad habits are easy to form but hard to live with."

Create a Positive Affirmation

Write down your new habit as a statement. The way you phrase it is, "I am always (punctual) for every appointment." You write it as a positive, present tense, personal affirmation. "I always arise by 6:00 am every morning." Write it in the present tense as though it were already true.

When you write it down in this way, and frame it in these words, your subconscious mind accepts this as a command and begins to adjust your behavior at an unconscious level so that it is consistent with your new command. Your subconscious ability to command yourself to develop new habits is one of the most powerful faculties that you have.

Reprogram Yourself for Success

Determine three actions you can take to develop your new habit. For example, a person who wants to start getting up earlier might set his alarm to go off early and then place it on the other side of the room, so that when it goes off, he has to get up and cross the room to turn it off. He could even put his lights on a timer so that the alarm goes off and the lights come on at the same time.

Visualize yourself as if you already had the new habit. Create a mental picture of yourself with this habit. Imagine how you would walk, talk, and act. You direct a movie in your mind, and see yourself with this habit.

When you visualize yourself with your new habit, your subconscious mind believes that you are actually doing what you are visualizing. When you visualize a new behavior over and over, your subconscious mind records this as a new action each time. In no time at all, your new behavior becomes automatic.

Practice Positive Self Talk

Affirm and talk to yourself as if you already had this habit. Be your own cheerleader. Say, "Boy, I like being punctual. I'm punctual all the time. I never miss an appointment. I leave early so I can always be on time. I have a great reputation for punctuality. People look up to me because I'm so punctual. People use me as their role model."

In other words, talk to yourself the way you want to be sometime in the future. Over time, you will actually become that kind of person—and sometimes far faster than you imagined.

Act As If

Another way to develop a new habit is to "act as if you already had this habit." The more you act as if, visualize it and affirm your new behavior, the faster you program your new behavior into your subconscious until it becomes automatic.

Think about a single habit that you would like to develop. What one habit is within your reach? What one habit could you start practicing immediately? Pick something that is reasonable; something that you can be successful at.

Here's an interesting psychological principle. If you select a simple habit and you practice it until it becomes easy and automatic, your self-confidence increases dramatically, making you eager to develop the next new habit. Soon, you'll be setting goals to establish new habits in your life that you might have never thought possible.

Write down three actions that you can take each day to develop or practice this habit. Then ask yourself what one action you're going to take immediately to develop one habit that can help you right now.

How Rich People Think

This brings us to another whole body of thought; about how rich people think. Lots of research has been done in this area. There are dozens of differences between rich people and poor people; between upper classes and middle classes and lower classes. As we said, you become what you think about most of the time.

So, the way you think on the inside determines what happens to you on the outside. If you think the way rich people think, you will soon get the results that rich people get.

When I began to teach about self-made millionaires I continued to do more research. I kept coming across little one-liners; little ideas. An example is that wealthy people develop the habit of doing the things that poor people don't like to do. So the question then was what are these things that poor people don't like to do? The answer is that they are the same things that rich people don't like to do either. Isn't that a great one-liner?

But rich people do them because they know that's the price of becoming financially successful. They get up earlier. They work harder. They stay later and they spend more time studying and growing. They sacrifice, sometimes for months and years. They work 60 or 70 hours a week. They don't really like doing this, but they know that's the price that you pay.

Rich people make a habit of doing the things that poor people don't like to do.

Long-Term versus Short-Term Thinking

Rich people have three special ways of thinking. The first special way of thinking is long-term thinking versus short-term thinking. The great majority of people, 80%, think short-term. They think about immediate gratification. They think about immediate happiness and satisfaction. They think about eating whatever they want to eat and about watching television and socializing with their friends.

Today, one of the great killers of success is electronic distractions. People allow themselves to be distracted by their smart phone, the internet and social media, along with texting, all day long. They become like attention deficit disorder children—they can't stay on task and they get very little work done. These distractions just continue all day long once they start first thing in the morning. Why? It's because a distraction gives a person a certain amount of pleasure.

The pleasure is caused by a jolt of dopamine which is released by the brain whenever you experience a stimulus of any kind. Dopamine stimulates the same receptors as cocaine does. When you respond to an electronic interruption—any bing, buzz or jingle of some kind—it triggers the release of dopamine in your brain and it gives you a small lift or jolt. Eventually, people can become addicted to this tiny little buzz every time they receive or send an email or electronic message of any kind.

They did a study recently and found that university students check their Facebook accounts up to 18 times an hour. Think about that! If you are in a normal working environment, you must be very cautious, because you'll often be checking your email or social media accounts up to ten or 20 times an hour. If that's the case, you're finished. You can never get anything done of any value. You can never learn or retain anything and you won't be able to complete major tasks because all learning requires extended periods of study. All major tasks require extended periods of concentrated, focused hard work.

So, most people have short-term thinking. People with short-term thinking seek immediate gratification rather than delayed gratification.

Dr. Edward Banfield did 50 years of research at Harvard University and found that the one single factor that was more responsible for upward socio-economic mobility—the sociological term for "getting rich," was that wealthy people thought long-term. They were willing to make investments today that might take three to five years to complete, and then another five years to become profitable. But in the second ten years of the process, they could make millions of dollars.

Just think about building a restaurant. It might take two or three or four years with design and approvals and investment, and then perfecting all the operating requirements, and may cost one to five million dollars. But once a really good restaurant is up and running, that restaurant can be full and sending tens of thousands of dollars in revenues to the owners every single day.

Think of a factory that may take five or six years to plan, build and organize. Once it's working it can produce hundreds or thousands of products generating profits.

So, think long-term. The key to thinking long-term is really simple: set goals, for five and ten years from now. One of the things that I encourage people to do is say, "If I could wave a magic wand and my life would be perfect in five years, what would it look like? What would I be doing and how much would I be earning? What kind of standard of living would I have? What kind of home would I live in? Who would I be working with? What kind of health would I have?

Always project forward five years. Ken Blanchard, author of *The One Minute Manager*, calls this a five year fantasy. And you'll find that successful people who think long-term are always projecting forward five years. They're willing to make sacrifices in the short-term to enjoy greater rewards in the long-term.

Slow versus Fast Thinking

The next type of thinking that top people use is slow thinking versus fast thinking. The Nobel Prize winning neuropsychologist, Daniel Kahneman wrote a book recently called, *Thinking Fast and Slow*. The book became a worldwide bestseller and it has one great idea that causes it to deserve to be successful. The idea is that there are two types of thinking; fast thinking and slow thinking.

Fast thinking is sort of intuitive, automatic, instinctual, quick, thoughtless thinking. An example is when you're driving through traffic; you're thinking quickly. Or when you're in conversation with others, you're thinking fast. Fast thinking is quite appropriate for most everyday things.

The other type of thinking is slow thinking. Slow thinking is where you stop the clock, take time out, and really think carefully about what it is you're going to do or say, and what it is you need to decide upon for the long term.

Here is Kahneman's insight which makes it such a great piece of work. He said, "The big mistake that people make is that they use fast thinking when they should be using slow thinking."

An example is: if you're going to become a successful business person or a millionaire of billionaire, you're going to have to hire people. Peter Drucker once said that fast people decisions are invariably wrong people decisions. Now whenever I share that with business owners or managers, there's a collective groan in the audience because everybody recognizes that some of the biggest mistakes you make include getting involved with people quickly, without giving it enough time to think.

So the critical word here is: consequences. It's one of my favorite words. I've studied time management for 30 years, and very early in my studies I came across this word.

Something is important to the degree to which it has serious potential consequences. Something is unimportant to the degree to which it has low or no consequences. And so the things that have high consequences are things that require long-term and slow thinking.

For example, the career you choose, or the investment you make that you can't get out of for maybe five years. Other examples are: the person you marry, the company you start, the products and services you bring to market. The time to do the serious thinking is before you make the irrevocable decisions. This requires thinking long-term and it requires thinking slowly.

Informed Thinking

The third type of thinking that rich people use is called informed thinking versus uninformed thinking. That's what we talked about before. Rich people do a lot of work to get a lot of information on a subject before they make an irrevocable commitment to it. Inexperienced or poor people make decisions with very little information, and sometimes with almost no information at all. They make uninformed decisions.

So here is what we have found. The more time you take to gather information before you make an important long-term decision, the better that decision will be. Sometimes, at the end of the process, just one piece of information that you gather can change your mind completely about a course of action.

Take the time to do your homework. Take the time to do your due diligence. Take the time to get the facts. Harold Geneen, one of the great business conglomerators said that you must get the facts. "Get the real facts, not the assumed facts or the hoped for facts. The facts don't lie." He said that if you get enough facts, the right course of action will emerge like cream rises to the top of milk.

More Ways Rich People Think—Earning More Money

Let's talk about how rich people think. Number one, rich people think about earning more money. They think about that all the time. You can say that you think about earning more money. But what most people really think about is *having* more money. They don't think about *earning* more money.

So, how do you earn more money? The answer is for you to create value for someone else. You make sales or do something else that somehow benefits and enriches the lives of other people. You create and offer products and services that improve peoples' lives and work. Successful people have this obsession with creating value for other people, for which they accrue a commission, because everybody works on straight commission. So they are always looking at the landscape looking for a need that people have that they could fill, at a profit. And they think about this all the time.

Richard Branson has started around 82 businesses. Almost all of them have been successful. Some of those businesses failed and he was very thorough in dissecting the failures so that he didn't make the same mistakes again. But he has an enormous number of businesses and he's become one of the richest men in the world. Interestingly, he is dyslexic so he really can't read that well or follow information, so he hires people who can.

He was asked how it was that he could start and build so many successful businesses. He said, "Starting and building a successful business involves certain basic principles. Sort of like in math, where two and two is always four, two into four is two, and so on." He said, "Once you have the basic principles, and you've successfully built one business, you just replicate the principles over and over again in other businesses."

The one guiding factor for Richard Branson and other wealthy people is that they are always thinking about earning more money by providing more value to more people.

Leverage

The second way people think is, rich people think that leverage is the key to wealth. Average people, unfortunately, think that hard work is the key to wealth. You'll see a lot of this politically, where they try to make a big thing of the idea that people can't get ahead just through hard work. And no, they never could. If you just work hard and earn a paycheck, then you take it home and spend the money just to stay alive, paying for your home, your clothes, food, and so on.

What you have to do is accumulate money. The way you accumulate money is by sacrificing in the short-term, saving your money and avoiding immediate gratification, and then investing that money somewhere so that it gives you leverage. Leverage is how you multiply the money. It could be in buying or building a rental accommodation that yields you enough money to cover all the associated costs, plus a profit. But it does take money to make money.

However, here's an interesting rule. It does not have to be your money. If you can demonstrate that you have the ability to deploy money so that it in turn makes money, people will line up to give you money to deploy.

There is not really a shortage of money; there's only a shortage of ideas on how to create wealth. What sort of ways could you save and accumulate money, demonstrate to others that you are a good risk with that money, and then get leverage, so you can invest in something that gives you more and more cash.

Practical Experience Works

The third way that rich people think is that they believe in specific, practical ideas and experience as the keys to success. Average people think that formal education is the key to success. It's interesting that 54% of university graduates were still unemployed one year after leaving college last year. Eighty percent of university graduates never worked in the fields in which they graduated, for the rest of their lives.

Most of what is taught in universities doesn't involve ways to create more value and make more money. They teach theoretical subjects. Yet, many people are convinced that if they get a degree, then they will earn a lot of money.

It is true that people who are better educated do earn more money, but it's only because they have demonstrated that they have the intelligence to find a way to create value.

So what are the specific, practical ideas and experience that you need as the keys to success? Here's a question that I ask my audiences all the time. If you could wave a magic wand and be absolutely excellent at any one skill, what one skill would help you the most to double your income? It's the most amazing thing; almost everybody knows what that skill is. If you don't know what it is, you must find out. Ask your boss, your friends, your spouse and your coworkers.

"If I was really, really good at one thing, what one skill would help me the most to increase my income—to be more valuable and to make a greater contribution?" Then, whatever that skill is, you set down as a goal and you make a plan. You work on developing that skill every day.

One of the insights that changed my life, and was a turning point at the age of 24, was that you can learn anything you need to learn to achieve any goal you can set for yourself. You can learn anything you need to learn to earn more money. Everybody who is earning more money today was once earning less money.

I sometimes ask my audiences if they would like to double their income. Everybody always says yes. Then I tell them that if they want to double their income, to find someone who is earning twice as much as them and find out what they did, and what they're doing. And then do the same things. Remember that everybody who is earning twice as much as you today was at one time earning half as much. Then they started doing something differently from you, and now they're earning twice as much. Once you have learned how to double your income, then what do you do? Well, you learn how to double it again, and double it again.

The average person's income in our society goes up at about 3% per annum. Basically, just above the rate of inflation. However, wealthy people's income—people in the top 20%—enjoy increases of about 11% per annum. The difference is outlined in a University of Chicago study by Gary Becker, the Nobel Prize winning economist. He found that people in the bottom 80% were not increasing their knowledge and skills. They were coasting. The great tragedy is that there is only one direction in which you can coast, and that's downhill.

But people in the top 20% are continually learning, and upgrading their skills. People in the top 10% are increasing their incomes at 15% to 20% per year, and those in the top 5% increase their incomes at 25% and more.

Now, if you're in the top 5% of learners/earners, you'll double your income every 18 months, and once you've doubled your income, you do it again. The way you do that is by continuing to increase your value. You increase your ability to make a valuable contribution that other people will pay for.

How could you leverage your skills and your money and relationships to increase your earning ability? How could you leverage the things that you have today?

Money-Making Thinking

The fourth way that rich people think is they think about moneymaking activities. Average people think about pleasurable activities and fun activities, and so-cializing on the weekends and watching sporting events.

Successful people are always thinking about mon-ey-making activities. "What can I do to make money?" They enjoy the idea of creating value and making money.

What could be the most profitable activities for you to engage in? What could you do to earn money?

I'll give you a very simple example. I met an interest-ing couple at one of my seminars. They both worked for a large health care company. They both made a pretty good income. A few years before, they had taken a week-end seminar on what is called "buy 'em, fix 'em," where you would find a home that was underpriced relative to the market because it needed work. They would offer a lowball price and negotiate the lowest price they could get. If possible they would negotiate "no money down." Then they would offer to pay the seller off over five or ten years based on their equity plus a low rate of inter-est, and often get the house for no money down at all.

Then they would work on evenings and weekends to fix up the house and the landscaping. There are a number of renovations, beginning with kitchens and bathrooms that yield five or even ten dollars for every dollar you spend.

Then they would rent out the house for an amount that more than paid for the cost of the first mortgage which they now had, the second mortgage to the previous owner, plus a profit on the amount they had invested. Then they would move on.

They would increase the value of the property by about $50,000 each time. They told me the first time it took six months to get to the rental stage, their second house took four months, and the third took three months.

After a couple of years they were buying, fixing and renting out a house every month. How long do you think it would be before they became millionaires, and then multi-millionaires with no downside? With their tenants paying all the costs, any bank in town would give them all the money they would need to buy homes because they had such a high level of cash flow.

You may think that sounds like pretty simple stuff, and it is. Do you know that this technique has been one of the great sources of wealth in America and other countries for one hundred years? You could probably do it tomorrow yourself if you were willing to make the sacrifice of time and money and go out and look at houses until you find one that works. You put in your sweat equity; your physical rather than financial equity, and gradually build your operation up.

Is it easy? No. Your first house may take you six to 12 months to figure how to get it right. But then your second house is much faster, and your third house even faster. People get to do what they love, and they earn a lot of money from it.

Average people do work they don't like, and think that is the price they have to pay to survive. Rich people love to get to work. As a matter of fact, when they're not working they think about their work. They get up early in the morning because they want to get to work soon.

Here's a very simple way you can tell if you're going to be rich or not. It's called the clock test. The clock test asks what the clock means to you at work. For rich people, the clock is something they race against. They want to work; lots of work and then more work. They want to do better work, and the clock is ticking down and restricting the amount of time they have left to work. They are always competing against the clock.

How do poor people think about the clock? Poor people think of the clock as the enemy. It's the enemy because it sits there telling them when they have to start, when they can go home, and how long their coffee breaks and lunch breaks are.

You've heard the old saying, "I felt like the clock had stopped." Many people, from the time of about three in the afternoon, begin watching the clock. The clock tells them when they can stop working, and that's what they're looking forward to. Actually, all day they're watching the clock, and these people have no future.

If you're doing what you love to do, you race against the clock and you want to do more stuff that you enjoy, gets results, and makes you feel successful and happy. So how do you feel about your work?

What I've discovered is that there is a "right" job for you. There is probably more than one. You were born with special skills, talents and abilities that, taken together, nobody else has. You've had a combination of experience that is unique to you. Your job and great responsibility in life is to find the perfect place for yourself.

I've run large companies, have been a manager and have had people approach me for jobs. I still remember one guy coming in. He was in his 30s, was fit and well dressed, good looking and obviously well educated. He said that he was just looking for someone who would take him and help him and guide him and make him successful—someone who would be his coach, counselor and mentor and work with him for a few years.

And I said to him, "Good luck. Anybody who could do that is too busy doing what they enjoy doing to take your hand and coddle you. I get people all the time saying, 'Please, take me and guide me to do the right things to be successful and happy.' I say, this is your responsibility. As an adult, your responsibility is to find what a great spiritual teacher referred to as 'your true place.' Find your true place; the place that was meant for you—the place where you fit in naturally, like a key into a lock. When you find that place, you'll make more progress in a few months or years than many people make in a lifetime."

So just think about the clock. Do you look forward to getting up in the morning? Can you hardly wait to get to work? Do you hate to leave work? Do you love to work in the evenings and on weekends?

The most successful people I know have to practice the discipline of not working. They have to force themselves and fight with themselves not to work, because they enjoy working so much. Working gives them so much happiness and satisfaction.

Networking

Another way that rich people think is rich people believe in continually meeting new people and expanding their relationships. On the other hand, average people associate with the same people at work and after work and on weekends. Then they go home and watch television.

You've heard about the concept of networking. In fact, networking is one of the most important things that you do; getting out and meeting people face to face. There's a lot of talk today about social networking, and what we say is that social networking is social not working.

People do not make long-term valuable, deep relationships by sharing tidbits of information and photographs back and forth on the internet. People develop relationships by getting head to head, knee to knee, and face to face with other people who they can help, and who can help them.

Who are the kinds of people that you want to associate with? Who are the people in your industry or trade group or business that have something to offer you, and you have something to offer them? You'll find that the most successful people are those who are frequently at Chamber of Commerce meetings, real estate association meetings, business club meetings, Rotary, Kiwanis, Lions Club, and so on. They are constantly out and moving around, meeting new people, and asking them what they do. All of these organizations are looking for new people to join them.

The rule is that you should only join one or maybe two organization. That's enough. Go to a couple of association meetings and get a feel for the place. See if you like the organization and the people. I've had experiences where I thought of getting involved in an organization and went to a couple of meetings and found that I didn't care for them. I found the people boring or uninteresting, or I wasn't interested in the subjects they were focused on.

Find an association or group made up of people devoted to subjects that you care about. Once you've joined the association, find out how the whole thing works. Remember that every association does certain things and has various committees. Find out what these committees are and what they do, and then volunteer to help.

When you start to network with other people, instead of looking for what they can do for you, look for opportunities to do something for them. Volunteer your services to help on a particular committee.

Many years ago I was asked if I would get involved with the local Community Chest. This is a group that solicits money from a variety of different sources and then divides it up and hands it out to different worthy causes within the community. I agreed to offer my speaking services to help with their sales, marketing and personal development.

As a result, I got involved with about sixteen of the top business people in the community—people I could have never gotten to otherwise, as a young guy just starting off. But here they were—presidents and vice presidents of major organizations who had come together to work on this charitable function for a six month period. I worked very hard with them and then did business with those people for the next five years. The reason for this was that I got an opportunity to perform with these people; to make suggestions, do jobs, get results, and to report back. They began to notice me and it lead to my being hired to head up a $265 million dollar development company, and it changed my whole career.

The other thing is this: when you network with people, instead of looking for what's in it for you, look into what's in it for them. So you ask them what sort of work they do, and they'll tell you.

Then you ask them what you would have to know to send them a customer.

One of the very best things you can do in business to build goodwill is to send your new acquaintances a customer. And even if the customer doesn't buy, your new acquaintance will like and respect you, and will want to reciprocate by sending you a customer as well. Always ask what you can do for them.

Napoleon Hill said that we've gone from the age of the go getter to the go giver. So whenever you meet new people, always ask what you can do to help them. Ask yourself what resources you have available that may be of help to them in their work.

When you've met a new person, go home and think about how you can help that person. Maybe send them a book, a copy of an article, or an email saying how happy you were to meet with them and that you hope to see them again soon.

Remember that if you sow a lot of seeds, some of those seeds will bloom and grow. Sometimes one person that you meet at one networking function or association meeting can be a person that changes your life. Eighty-five percent of new job opportunities come about because one person introduces somebody they know to someone else. It's mostly not through advertising or sending applications or going for interviews. It's about somebody who knows somebody that can open a door.

Here's the rule: the more relationships you have; the more people you know and that know you in a positive way, the more opportunities you're going to have and the wealthier you're going to become.

Some years ago I met this young guy who had moved to a town knowing nobody. After a year, when I met him, he was in newspaper articles with photos and quotes. I asked him how he had gone from knowing no one in that large city to being talked about in the papers all the time. He said, "I never went home at night. Five days a week at least I went and found some association or meeting, even at lunch or dinner with people. I constantly got my face out there, talking to people and looking for ways to help them."

Within one year he had literally gone from being a nobody from nowhere to one of the most respected people in his community. He had job offers and investment opportunities coming in. I still remember what an amazing thing it was. His philosophy was very simply to get out and get among them. Don't go home and watch TV.

Belief in Quality

A seventh way that rich people think is they believe that outstanding performance and quality work are the keys to success. Average people believe that a secure job is the key to financial safety and security. Rich people believe that the key to success is to be really good at what you do. They are always upgrading their skills so that they do what they do in an excellent fashion.

Rich believe that quality work stands out above everything else and that people will remember it and talk about it. And that turns out to be true. There are very few rich people who do not have a reputation for being very good at what they do. They are usually in the top 10% in their field.

You don't have to be number one; you just have to be really good at what you do. Ask yourself, "What are you famous for?" If two people who know you were talking about you, what would they say about your skills and abilities and the quality of your work? How would they describe you? How would you like them to describe you at some time in the future?

You'll find that all successful people are described by others as being very good at what they do. They are excellent at their jobs. They are the kind of people that others want to hire. They are the go-to people, if you have a need of any kind. They cost more money, but they are worth vastly more than the small increment in price.

What are the things that you need to be really good at to get a reputation for high-quality work and out-standing performance? Dedicate yourself to becoming very, very good at what you do. Dedicate yourself to becoming the best at what you do. You want people to say, "There are lots of people who do this, but he or she is the best.

The 7 Basics of
Business Success

Let's talk now about the seven basics of business success. You see, financial success is usually based on starting, building, managing or turning a failing business around. Fully 90% of millionaires and billionaires either started a business or went to work for a business when it was small and then stayed with it as it grew. Most millionaires and billionaires earn their money in a business of some kind, and so can you.

1) Number one, which we talked about before is called "Find a need and fill it." What is it that people want and need and value, and are willing to pay for? Business success is the result of serving customers with products and services that they want and need and that can change and improve their life or work in some way.

What is the biggest need of your customers that you could satisfy today? What is the biggest problem for your customers that you could solve? Remember we said to find a big problem that a lot of people have and then solve it in a unique and different way.

2) The second basic of business success is that "The purpose of a business is to create and keep a customer." Profitability is not the purpose of a business. Profitability is the result of creating and keeping customers at a cost that is lower than acquiring and servicing new customers. All successful business people think about creating customers all the time. They think about what they can do to interest people so that they will buy and use their products and services. They know that if they do this well enough and often enough and cost effectively enough, that profit will be the automatic result.

How do you create and keep customers in your own line of work? Always ask if there could be a better way. Because the answer is that there is almost always a better way than the way you're doing it today.

3) The third basic of business success is that nothing happens until a sale takes place. As Peter Drucker said, "There are no results inside the business. All the results are outside the business. They are out there with the customer somewhere."

It's amazing to me how many people in business spend so much of their time inside their business sending out emails to try to get people to buy from them without ever going out and calling on real life customers to ask what they want and then show them that their product or service will give them that.

I was working with a great company and talking to the president. This was about a two billion dollar company with four thousand employees nationwide. It had started off at a kitchen table with this president and two other guys who were all salesmen. They had just been let go from their company because it had collapsed. They decided to start up a new company doing the same thing that they had just left and to do it better. And so they did. Today he flies around in a private jet, is extremely wealthy.

So I asked him how he would describe his job. He immediately said, "Chief Sales Officer." I said, "Chief Sales Officer?" He said, "Yes. When we sat at that kitchen table we agreed that I would be the CSO, not only the sales manager, but also the sales maker. From that day to this all I think about all day long is making sales."

So you could see why he and his company were so successful. They had 600 salespeople. These salespeople worked in every major community in America and Canada, and all they thought about all day long was making sales.

4) The number four basic of business success is there are only four ways to increase sales in your business, or in any other business. The first is to make more individual sales. You can find more individual customers. The second is to make larger sales to each customer. The third is to make more frequent sales to each customer, and often this is the breakthrough. The fourth way is to offer

new, different, and better products or services to each customer. Those are the only four ways.

How do you make more individual sales? How do you make larger transactions; to buy more, up-sell, and cross-sell? Third, how do you get people to keep coming back more often? Some of the most successful companies in the world are those that take such good care of their customers that they come back over and over again, and bring their friends. And then finally, what new or different products or services could you offer along with your current product line to your existing customers that they want and need, and are going to buy somewhere.

5) The fifth basic is that there are only four ways to change or improve your business results. Number one is to do more of certain things. The question you have to ask is what should you be doing more of if you want to increase your sales and profitability?

Number two is to do less of other things. What are the things that you need to do less of, say no to or diminish, so that you have more time to do more of the things that generate more sales and profitability?

The third way to change or improve your business is to start doing something new or different. And this is the hardest of all. Starting something new or different is really, really difficult. What is it that you need to start doing that you are not doing today? Where is it that you need to move out of your comfort zone? Doing something new or different involves risk because although there is the possibility of success, there is no certainty.

Thomas J. Watson Sr., the founder of IBM was once asked by a young journalist how he could be more successful faster. Watson said, "If you want to be more successful faster you must double your rate of failure." He said, "Success lies on the far side of failure. If you're not failing often enough then you are not succeeding fast enough."

The fourth thing you can do to change or improve is to stop doing certain things completely. Just stop them altogether. What we find is that there are certain things that you're doing that if you thought about it you would not have started doing them in the first place. You need to ask yourself what you need to stop doing so that you'll have more time to do other things.

6) This brings us to the sixth basic of business success, and that is to practice zero based thinking in all areas. Zero based thinking is one of the great thinking tools of successful and wealthy people. What you do is ask this question. "Is there anything you are doing today that you would not start again today if you could do it over, knowing what you now know?"

Sometimes I call this a KWINK analysis—Knowing What I Now Know. You apply this to your relationships. Are there any relationships, business or personal, that knowing what you now know, you wouldn't get involved with them again today if you had to do it over?

When I work with managers I say "Is there anyone working for you who, knowing what you now know, you would not hire them back again today? If they walked in today to apply for their current job, you would not hire them based on your knowledge of how they perform." If the answer is yes then the next question is how do you get rid of them, and how fast?

The second area to apply zero based thinking is in business activities. Is there anything you're doing in your business that knowing what you now know, you wouldn't start up again today? Are there any products that you would not bring to the market today, knowing what you now know? Are there any services that you would not offer to your customers today, knowing what you now know? Are there any business processes, methods, activities, or expenses that knowing what you now know, you wouldn't start them up again today? If there is something you would not start again today, the next question is "How do I get out of this and how fast." Cut it off immediately. Cut your losses as fast as you can.

The third area apply zero based thinking has to do with investments of time, money, and emotion. Human beings hate to lose anything. As a matter of fact, the fear of loss is twice or three times as great as the desire for gain. We hate to admit if we have invested a lot of time and it has not worked out. So what we do is throw good time after bad. We throw good money after bad. We try to recoup the amount of time we've lost by investing more time, when the real thing we should do is to stop altogether. We may have invested a lot of money in a course of action, product or investment. But knowing what we now know, we wouldn't invest that money.

Then the only question is "How do you get out, and how fast?

Finally, emotion is another investment. We invest a lot of emotion in another person, a career or course of action. I had a terrible time when I encouraged several of my friends to get involved with me in a business that didn't work out, and I felt absolutely terrible about it, until I found that my friends didn't care. But the emotion of getting myself and other people involved can cause you to keep doing it over and over, even though you know you wouldn't ever get into it again if you had to do it over.

Here's an exercise for you. What one action are you going to take immediately as the result of your answers to this zero based thinking question? What is it in your life that you're going to stop doing altogether because knowing what you now know you would never have gotten into it?

7) The seventh basic in business is that change is the most important factor determining your success in business. There are three factors that are driving change today. The first is knowledge, which is increasing daily in every area, and one new piece of knowledge can completely transform your business, markets and your customers.

Second is technology, which is changing entire industries overnight. Every new advance in technology is being picked up by other people and multiplied by other advances in technology. Technological advances are growing faster today than we ever thought possible.

The third factor of change is competition. Your competitors are more skilled, determined and aggressive than ever before. They are thinking 24 hours a day about how to take away your customers by offering your customers better, faster, cheaper, easier and more convenient products and services to enhance their lives and work.

My little equation says that Knowledge (K) multiplied by Technology (T) multiplied by Competition (C) equals ROC, which is Rate of Change. Is the rate of change going to be faster or slower tomorrow? The answer is that the rate of change in every field is accelerating and is never going to slow down. When things change your ability to accept, adapt and adjust, roll with and do new things is absolutely essential for your success.

So keep asking, "If I was not doing things this way, knowing what I now know, would I do them now keeping in mind the rates of change in information, technology and competition?"

Here are some questions for you. What effect are these factors of change having on your business? How is the information and knowledge explosion affecting your business today? Where is it coming from and what difference is it making? Are you keeping current? What kinds of technology changes are affecting your business today? What is your competition doing to serve their customers better and faster by using new technology? What is your competition doing in general with regard to change? There are many books on this subject along with multi-semester courses at leading universities on competitive strategy and advantage.

In business you must always be looking over your shoulder to see what your competitors are doing or what they are likely to do. You remember when Apple introduced the first iPhone in 2006 and Blackberry dismissed it as a toy? "Nobody wants apps, they said. It's just a passing fad." Nokia also dismissed the iPhone in the same way, and both of those companies lost massive amounts of market share nearly overnight. What changes are taking place on your landscape and among your competition that you're going to have to adapt to very quickly?

Charles Darwin was famous for saying that the contest of survival goes not to the strongest or most intelligent of the species, but to the one most adaptive to change. That applies to you and me as well.

The 7 Habits of
High-Profit Businesses

Many thousands of businesses have been studied around the world for many years to determine the factors that most predict growth and profitability. Here are the seven most important factors.

1) The most successful and profitable companies offer high quality products and services. High quality products and services are always defined in terms of what your customer considers to be quality and value. For example, Walmart, the biggest retail operation in the world. What do its customers, people who live from paycheck to paycheck, consider to be quality and value? For them it means a wide selection of guaranteed products at everyday low prices. That makes Walmart the biggest retail operation in history.

Tiffany & Co. is different. They offer high-quality jewelry for a particular type of customer. Lululemon offers specialty clothing for a particular and discerning customer base. So you have to ask yourself, "Who are my customers and what do they consider to be quality?" Top companies are recognized as superior to their competition in important areas.

Top companies invest in Continuous and Never Ending Improvement—(CANEI). They are never satisfied because they know that their competitors are working day and night to put them out of business by coming up with improvements that will make their products preferable to your products and services.

Harvard University has been doing a study known as PIMS—Profit Implication of Market Strategies. They've been doing it for many years, first with hundreds and now thousands of companies to try to determine the market strategies that lead to the greatest profitability. Here's what they found.

Companies that are known for high quality are also the highest profit companies in their industries. Companies that are known for low quality are in the lowest profit group, and the worst of these usually go out of business.

Inc. Magazine did the study of the Inc. 500 last year and they looked at the very best way that a company could invest money to grow, and found that it was not in advertising or marketing of any kind. The very best place to invest company money was in improving the quality of the product in the first place. This would have a greater impact on sales and profitability than anything else.

2) The second habit of high profit businesses is that they develop a complete business plan before starting, and continually upgrade their plan when the market changes. Most business people are impatient with business planning, but it's an essential part of business success. It forces you to think through each of the most important areas of your business before you commit time and treasure to that area.

Alan Lakein, the time management specialist said that "Action without thinking is the cause of every failure." This means that action preceded by thinking, especially thinking on paper, is the cause of every success. Successful businesses do complete market research to determine that there exists a profitable demand for their product or service,

Forbes Magazine recently reported that the number one reason, greater than all other reasons put together, why companies fail is because there's no real market demand for what they produce. They spend a lot of time investing in and developing products or services without ever going and finding if there is a real customer need or demand for them.

A friend of mine is a very successful woman and investor. She was approached by two women who had developed the most fabulous baby food. It had the highest proteins, carbohydrates, vitamins, minerals and so on. They wanted her to invest in their baby food company. So she said "Sure, give me some samples and I'll take them home." She had three children under the age of five at home. When she served the product to her children they spat it out all over the floor. The women who had developed this baby food had never tested it with a baby, and they lost all their money because kids wouldn't eat the food.

It's like the company that spent a fortune on the best dog food in the history of the world but failed because dogs hated it. So you've really got to be sure that there's a demand for your product or service before you produce the product or launch the marketing.

The third important part of this business planning habit is that successful businesses get accurate costs and prices to assure that profits are possible. It's so important that you do your homework. You do not assume that prices are going to be what they are. You double check and you get bids from different suppliers for your product components so that when you start to set sell prices on your product—prices that customers will actually pay, you know all of your costs exactly so that you know you can make a profit.

3) The third habit of successful businesses is that they have competent managers and staff at all levels of the business. They are known for being a place where good people work. They hire very, very carefully. They know that 95% of business success is determined by the skills, abilities and personalities of the people who work for them.

I was talking to a very wealthy businessman a couple of days ago and he was saying that the only limit on the growth of his business is finding competent people.

I've found this to be true myself over the years. The only limits on the growth of your business are first of all your competence as a businessman, and second, your ability to attract other competent people who can work with you. The best companies set high standards of performance. They hire better people and they replace poor performers.

In fact, in a study of the most successful companies in 22 countries, they found there were three qualities that stood out. Number one, they had clear goals and objectives for the company, for every department, and for every person in every department.

Number two, they had clear measures and standards for performance and deadlines, for every person and for every job.

Number three, they paid very well for exceptional performance. It turned out that those three qualities; clear goals, clear measures and standards, and excellent rewards for high performance were more predictive of business success than any other factors.

4) The fourth habit of business success is that top businesses develop an excellent marketing plan to attract a continuous flow of new customers. Their advertising is positive, attractive and aimed at their best potential customers.

This is an important point. The key to marketing success is knowing exactly who your customer is and especially who your ideal customer is. You need to know the demographics of your ideal customer—their age, education, income, family formation, and so on.

You also need to know the psychographics—the wants, doubts, fears, hopes, dreams and goals. You need to know the ethnographics—how they use your product or service and what role your product or service plays in their lives. Only when you know these things can you effectively promote to exactly those people who most want the benefits your product or service offers more than anyone else, and are willing to pay for it.

Sometimes, when I am meeting with business people I will say, "Describe to me your perfect customer; the one who wants and needs and is willing to buy your product, faster and easier and with fewer objections than anyone else. Don't tell me what your product is and don't tell me about your company or industry. Just describe the person."

This is a great exercise for you in business. You think through who that customer is exactly. Sometimes this is called the avatar; the one person that summarizes all the best qualities and characteristics of your perfect customer. Then you think about what you need to do to find those people, appeal to them, and get them to try your product or service.

At the best companies, the cost of acquiring new customers is lower than the profits they earn from them. All of business comes down to one thing. It's buying customers. Everything you do in your business is an expense aimed at buying a customer who will buy more from you and yield more profit to you than the cost of acquiring the customer in the first place. If you can acquire customers at a lower cost than profit, you can grow forever. Whenever you see a company that is in trouble, their costs of acquiring customers are greater than the profits they earn from them and the end is in sight.

Here's an exercise: What could you do immediately to improve the effectiveness of your marketing and advertising?

5) The fifth habit of business success is that successful businesses have an excellent sales process that consistently converts interested prospects into paying customers. This means that they have developed a step by step sales process from the first customer contact to the completed sale. Once they have this process they carefully hire and train excellent salespeople. Companies today succeed or fail based on the sales effort.

One of the big mistakes I see is that many people start and build companies without any experience in sales. As a result, they think that sales are like dew in the morning; just a natural process. All you do is create a product and then just hire salespeople and sell lots of it and take the money to the bank. These people are absolutely shocked at how hard it is to get a customer for the first time. They can't believe how hard it is to get a prospect to buy their product when they're already happy using somebody else's. It's one of the hardest aspects of business and it takes tremendous talent and skill.

Here's a question: What can you do immediately to improve the quality of your sales process?

6) The sixth habit of excellent businesses is that they have an excellent customer service plan to assure high levels of customer satisfaction and repeat business. They have a written plan to take care of their customers and to assure customer loyalty. More and more of their sales come from repeat customers and referrals.

We say that in business you have three goals. Number one is to get a potential customer to buy from you rather than from someone else. Number two is to take such good care of that customer that they come back and buy from you again and again.

And number three is to give such good customer service that your customers bring their friends to buy from you as well.

We live today in what we call the "recommendation nation." The success of a business is totally determined by the recommendations and referrals that you get from other people who are so happy they bought from you that they insist that their friends buy from you as well.

Sometimes I'll ask a room full of business, "What would happen to your business if you still had every customer that you ever had?" This always stops the conversation. "Gee," they say; "If I still had every customer I ever had I'd be rich."

Well then, the next question is, "What would you have to do with each customer you get from now on to make sure that they never go anywhere else?" The most successful companies like Apple—the highest capitalization company in the world—has customers that keep coming back to buy more and more stuff. The reason is that they are so happy with the previous products.

7) The seventh habit of successful businesses is that they have excellent systems in place to assure maximum efficiency and quality at the lowest costs. They have written job descriptions and clear procedures for every part of their business. Each person knows exactly how to do their job and their most important tasks.

When a business starts off, everybody does everything. But as the business grows, they have to stop the clock; take a time out, and write down step by step how each job is meant to be done. Each customer contact has to be carefully organized and agreed upon so that everybody says the same words to every customer at every point of contact. Each system in accounting, billing, shipping, handling, delivery and in customer relationships is written down clearly.

Here's what we suggest that you do. If you have a business and have certain procedures that you do repeatedly, sit down with a piece of paper and imagine you were explaining step by step to anew employee, exactly how it is done in this area.

Then make sure that they memorize the steps and follow them. This is how companies grow—by codifying processes and systems so that new people can come on and be brought up to speed and do an excellent job throughout.

Here's an exercise. What could you do immediately to assure greater clarity and better performance from your staff? How could you make sure that everybody is doing their job better and better, and enjoying it more?

Finally, what one habit of business success, based on these seven that we've been talking about, are you going to begin practicing immediately?

The 7 Habits for Personal Success

This brings us to the seven habits for personal success, and these are true in any field, but especially if you want to earn a lot of money and become a millionaire or even more in the course of your working lifetime.

1) Number one is the habit of daily goal setting. Many years ago I discovered this idea of daily writing out my major goals the things I needed to do to achieve them, and it transformed my life.

More than 85 % of wealthy people have one big goal that they are working on and they write it down and think about it and review it all the time.

The more you drive your major goal deep into your subconscious mind, the more you will activate your superconscious mind, your creativity and all of your other abilities for goal attainment.

Remember that your goals must be in writing. Only three percent of adults have written goals that they work at on a regular basis, and they earn ten times as much as people without written goals. This applies to people from the same schools, education, background, and the same opportunities.

We talk today about the one percent versus the 99%. But no, it's the three percent with goals versus the 97% who don't have any goals. Those are the people who have all the money and continually earn more.

You must read and review your goals daily, just as you would check a roadmap or your GPS if you were on a long distance trip cross-country. The real key is to do something every day to achieve your most important goal. Seven days a week, keep the plates spinning and do something every day.

2) The second habit for personal success is the habit of daily planning. What this means is that you make a list before you begin each day. You always work from a list. You can increase your productivity, performance and output by 25 to 50 percent, the day you start working from a list all day long.

Once you have a list you set clear priorities on your list. One of the things we encourage people to do is the ABCDE method. A is something you must do. B is something that you should do. C is something that would be nice to do but is not that important. D is something you delegate. E is something you eliminate

So set clear priorities on your list, and ask yourself this question. If I could only do one thing on this list before I was called out of town for a month, which one job would I want to be sure to get done? Put a circle around that and it becomes your top priority. Then start to work on that top priority.

Remember that the key to success is to set priorities and live by them. The key to failure is to not have priorities at all and be constantly distracted by everything that happens in your environment.

If you can determine your top priority and start to work on that every morning first thing, you'll double your productivity, performance and income faster than you can imagine.

3) The third habit of personal success is the habit of focus and concentration. These are the keys to great success. Every great accomplishment has been preceded by a long period of focused concentration over a long period of time.

Select your most important task; your top priority today, or your top priority in your life, work, family or health, and then begin working on it first thing. In your work life, you pick up that task and then you concentrate single-mindedly on it until it is 100% complete.

Here is a great discovery in success habits. If you start and complete an important task first thing each morning, you will step on the accelerator of your own potential. You will unlock your creative powers. You will kick yourself into flow, or give yourself an endorphin rush that makes you feel more powerful, more energetic, more creative and more motivated to do even more things.

You see, all of success is based on task completion. If you start and complete a task it gives you a buzz, makes you happy and exhilarated. If you start and complete a more important task you get more of a buzz. But if every morning you start and complete your most important task, it actually gives you an endorphin rush and you feel great all day long.

If you can develop the habit of starting and completing one important task each morning, you are going to become extraordinary at what you do, and your chances of becoming wealthy are going to go up like a rocket.

4) The fourth habit for personal success is the habit of continuous learning. The rule is very simple; read 30 to 60 minutes each day in your field. Keep expanding your knowledge in your field.

Secondly, listen to educational audio programs in your car and on your smart phone, or when you exercise. Turn traveling time and transition time into learning time. Turn your car into a university on wheels.

Always be learning new things—even if you only listen for five or ten minutes at a time, sometimes you'll get an insight that when added to your current knowledge can be priceless.

Attend every seminar and workshop that you can in your field. First of all, the very best and smartest people in your field speak at seminars and workshops. Second of all, the people who are at the seminars and workshops are some of the smartest and best people for you to know, meet and talk to. You can learn more at a good convention, seminar or workshop in a few hours or a couple of days than you could learn on your own in months and years of study and practice.

I find, as a seminar speaker, that it's always the top people that attend. It's also these same top people who come back again. The most interesting thing is that they come back and tell me their stories. Invariably, when they came to their first seminar they were struggling, and in many cases someone else had to pay for them to attend because they couldn't afford it. Now they're doing better, and the next time they're doing way better, and the next time they're rich. Eventually they have their own companies and recently, two guys who came to my seminar when they were penniless brought 38 members of their staff from their seven-state company.

They said, "Your seminar made us rich." So be aggressive about investing in yourself and in learning new skills.

5) The fifth habit for personal success, as we talked about earlier, is the habit of maintaining excellent health. In terms of diet, eat healthy and nutritious foods and refuse to eat foods that are not really great for you.

You know the rule is, if you want to be successful physically, eat less and exercise more. And if you're going to eat less, eat better and again, exercise more. Try to get 200 minutes of exercise each week and get seven to eight or more hours of sleep each night.

Remember that your brain is like a battery and it gets drained over the course of the day. The more you can recharge your brain by getting lots of sleep, the more powerful you'll feel all day long.

6) The sixth is the habit of hard work. Hard work, as we said right at the very beginning, is the distinguishing habit of successful people. Not just hard work but smart work as well. So start an hour earlier each day. Get up by 6:00 am and get moving. Work one hour longer each day. When everyone else goes home, stay there and get all of your work cleaned up.

Remember to "work all the time you work." I think this is one of the greatest success principles ever discovered. Don't waste time. When you go to work, just work. Don't chat with your friends, drink coffee, surf the internet, read the paper or go shopping during the daytime. When you work put your head down like a runner coming off the blocks at the Olympics, and just work all the time you're at work.

Imagine that they're going to do a special in your company to determine the hardest worker, and nobody knows about this study except you. Your job is to win the contest. Your job is to be acknowledged by everybody as the hardest worker in the company.

Hard work will do more to bring you to the attention of people who can help you than anything else you can do in your career. Unlike many things, it's totally under your control.

The average person today wastes fully 50% of working time, mostly in idle chitchat with coworkers and in activities that have nothing to do with the work. Instead, you work all the time you work. When you get there you smile at people and when they ask if you have a minute to talk, you tell them "Yes, but not right now. Right now I've got to get back to work. Let's talk after work."

7) Finally, number seven is the habit of continuous action. Move fast when you have an opportunity. Don't wait and don't delay. Make more sales calls. See more people. Study more information. Develop a fast life tempo. Be quick and in motion all the time.

Most importantly, develop a sense of urgency. Only two percent of people have a sense of urgency. That two percent are known and admired by everyone. They accomplish more. They attract more opportunities to themselves. People will give them more jobs and they become the go-to people in their operations. Everybody around them knows that if you want it done; give it to him or her.

Finally, I want to leave you with this key point. It is Goethe's wonderful quote: "Everything is hard before it becomes easy." Is it easy for you to become an absolutely exceptional person? Of course it's not. It's so hard to do. But it is possible.

You just do it a step at a time. Remember the old saying, "By the yard it's hard, but inch by inch, anything's a cinch." Make a decision right now that you are going to develop the qualities, the habits, the characteristics and the personality qualities of the most successful people, and then you're going to build your business so that it is one of the most successful businesses in the world. And I hope that you do.

Printed in the USA
CPSIA information can be obtained
at www.ICGtesting.com
JSHW012044140824
68134JS00033B/3253